Fran Bushe

Ad Libido

Additional Lyrics by Ben Champion

Salamander Street

PLAYS

First published in 2021 by Salamander Street Ltd, 272 Bath Street,
Glasgow, G2 4JR, info@salamanderstreet.com / www.salamanderstreet.com

PB ISBN: 9781914228391

BIOGRAPHY

Fran Bushe is an award-winning comedian, writer and performer. She has had sold-out runs and a UK tour of her multi-award-winning show *Ad Libido*, and wrote *The Diary of My Broken Vagina* for Channel 4 Comedy in 2019. Her book *My Broken Vagina* was published in 2021 by Hodder Studio. Fran has written sketches for Comedy Central and her play *Alive Day* is published in *20 Short Plays with Big Roles for Women*. She is an Associate Artist of Pleasance theatre and teaches sketch comedy and stand up.

Fran has spent years 'boning up' on sex. She has spoken with leading researchers, pleasure coaches and interviewed a growing number of people about their sexual experiences. It has also meant flustering many helpful members of staff at The British Library, with endless requests for books on the clitoris. She's popped crystals in her vagina, attended a vulva massage workshop and visited a sex camp where she had her 'Yoni' (...vagina) worshipped. Her candid approach to discussing sex and pleasure has led to her speaking with BBC Woman's Hour, Cosmopolitan and Jameela Jamil's 'I Weigh'. In 2018 she won Performer of the Year at the Sexual Freedom Awards (the statuette of which is a large golden winged phallus, which lives on her parents' mantlepiece).

Ad Libido started life on a Bryony Kimmings autobiographical theatre workshop and was first scratched at Battersea Arts Centre. It was then further developed at Pleasance Theatre (Litmus Fest), and Fran worked on the piece as part of her residencies at Theatre Deli and Arts Depot. *Ad Libido* is supported by Arts Council England.

Creative Team at the time of publishing:

Writer and performer	Fran Bushe
Director	Ellen Havard
Sound Designer	Annie May Fletcher
Composer and Additional Lyrics	Ben Champion
Set Design	Lizzy Leech
Lighting Associate	Joseph Ed Thomas
Choreographer	Sarah Blanc
Producer	Daisy Hale
Line Producer	Sean Brooks
Stage Manager	Frances Allison
Poster Design	Alex Powell
Photographer	Lidia Crisafulli

CHARACTERS

FRAN

EX

RECEPTIONIST

DOCTOR

PEOPLE

DOCTOR CHRISTIAN

INTERNET

PAULO

DOLPHIN GOD

SEX CAMP

FRIEND

FRAN'S LOVER

LEADER

MAN

MEN

YONI

All characters are all played by one person, however multi-roling could also be an option.

Preset: Onstage are two microphones (one downstage left, one downstage right). Centre stage is a projector screen covered in a gold sparkly curtain. **FRAN** *is offstage.*

FRAN: Please put your hands together, go wild, whoop, cheer and welcome to the stage Fran Bushe.

> **FRAN** *runs onstage and stands at stage right microphone. She switches between herself and the character of an ex-boyfriend.*

EX: "I heard you're making a show about sex Fran."

FRAN: "Oh. Hi ex-boyfriend from the past. Yeah, it's a theatre show, with songs."

EX: "*We've* had sex Fran."

FRAN: "Yeah."

EX: "So... the show is about me?"

FRAN: "No!"

EX: "But *we've* had sex Fran."

FRAN: "Yes…"

EX: "So, I'm in the show?"

FRAN: "No, no, nope, not at all. It's not a kiss and tell. The show is actually about me, imagine that. You're not in the show, no."

EX: "*Mmmmm.* Why not? Put me in the show. I think my skills should be immortalized through theatre."

> **FRAN** *covers microphone.*

FRAN: This is a real-life genuine conversation with a real live genuine ex boyfriend.

> **FRAN** *uncovers microphone.*

EX: "I mean give me my anonymity, my sense of mystique but say like the cool one, with a beard, that works in Theatre."

FRAN: "That actually doesn't whittle you guys down at all."

EX: "And let me know if you want any anecdotes, or hey, you are going to need a director, or maybe a little reminder, of my *skills*."

FRAN: "Your skills? I'll let you know."

FRAN walks to the middle of the stage and speaks to the audience.

FRAN: If you ever want your exes to get in touch, put on a show about sex and they will call. They will *all* call. But this show isn't about them. This show is about me and about sex. My name is Fran. I'm 31. I'm a writer. On forms I tick the heterosexual box and I have a vagina. Whoooo! You are going to be hearing a lot about my vagina during this show.

Everything I tell you is completely true, unless I tell you it isn't true and I will always say if it isn't true.

I've been sexually acting for as long as I've been sexually active, but the truth is I find sex hard, both in relationships and now as a single person, well, it's one thing saying to someone you love 'I'm not enjoying sex' and something very different saying it to someone you just met. So last summer I decided I was going to Fix Sex and I knew exactly where to begin. Hit it!

*'Funkytown' by Lipps Inc. plays. It fades down for **FRAN** to talk over.*

FRAN begins to do large lunges and generally warm up her pelvic region.

FRAN: Ok, I was ready, I was feeeeeling good, I was wearing my dungarees of sexual satisfaction and ding ding I'd caught the early bus to allow for significant travel delays. I'm visualising a successful and more sexually confident me. I *can* fix sex. I *will* fix sex!

She practices going through the motions of meeting the doctor.

FRAN: Hello, my name is Fran and I'm here to fix sex, no, sorry, Hi my name is Fran Bushe and I'm ready to fix sex.

To herself.

FRAN: Except I shouldn't call it 'sex', I should call it: full penetrative sex, no, intercourse, bonking? Banging? Making love? Making whoopie? Making the beast with two backs?

FRAN mime kicks down the imaginary door of the doctor's surgery.

RECEPTIONIST: "Are you here for the Doctor?"

FRAN: "Yes and it's about full penetrative sex – I would like to see The Sex Doctor please."

RECEPTIONIST: "Will your regular GP do?"

FRAN: "That'd be lovely thanks." Ok Fran, it's just your regular GP, who also treats your mum and your dad and also…

DOCTOR: "Sorry for the wait, there's been an emergency, what can I do for you?"

> **FRAN** *is suddenly nervous.*

FRAN: "I'm here about *not* enjoying sex, I don't think it's a medical emergency, I don't think anyone's ever died from not having sex. Has anyone ever died from not having sex? The last time I came I was 21, not *came* sexually you understand, came to the doctors about this specific problem and now I'm 31 and I'm ready to fix sex."

FRAN: *(To audience.)* I do a little buck up yeeha gesture here, I think it's because I want the doctor to have a nice time doctoring me.

FRAN: "I'm just not enjoying sex."

DR: "How does your partner feel about this?"

FRAN: "Oh well, I'm actually dating a few–"

DR: "Must be hard for him, let's see if we can book you in for couples' psychosexual therapy."

FRAN: "It might be a little bit intense to say "do you want to have sex... therapy with me" on a second date. We were just going to go to Pizza Express."

DR: "Perhaps you should schedule an appointment when you have a more regular committed partner."

FRAN: "And until then."

DR: "Have you ever tried MASTURBATION?"

FRAN: "Yes!"

DR: "What about just not having sex?"

FRAN *speaks to the audience.*

FRAN: As I left the room the doctor said

DR: "Good luck!"

FRAN: I'd come to the doctor for help. I was hoping that things had improved since the last time I'd been, because in that time we as a species have transplanted people's faces and brought the woolly mammoth back from extinction and I really didn't think I was asking for something radical.

DR: "Good luck!"

FRAN: Isn't something you say to someone whose come to you for help.

DR: "Good luck!"

FRAN: Feels like I'm completely on my own. And yes, I could try not having sex, I'd definitely be happier during and after sex if I wasn't having sex. So yeah, there is that. But some people, maybe even some people in this very room can come from just thinking about coming. Give it a go, I will happily wait. And others can come from watching horses race – that is why horse racing is so enduringly popular. And then there's the Extended Massive Orgasm, which is up to 100 orgasms in one session of sex, which sounds exhausting, and a bit greedy, share it out. But I would be so up for that. And dolphins right. Fuck the dolphins. They are one of the only other animals on the planet that enjoys sex for pleasure. They wrap eels and squids around their genitals to masturbate. They really do that; I saw it on a very blue episode of Blue Planet. If I was a dolphin, I'd spend a third of my life having and loving sex. Smug fucking dolphins!

SONG: **Smug Fucking Dolphins**

> *The dolphin who works at my gym*
> *Comes every time she takes a swim*
> *She says she squirts if you rub her fin*
> *Ok dolphins, you fucking win*
> *I wish I was a dolphin.*

Smug fucking dolphins fucking
Smug fucking dolphins fucking dolphins
Smug fucking dolphins fucking
Smug fucking dolphins smugly bumping ugly's
I wish I was a dolphin

The dolphins say it's a crime
If the earth doesn't move every single time
We should all be turned on from dusk till dawn
Not only when watching hard-core prawn
I wish I was a dolphin

Cos 'dolphin noise' means I'm in your net
'Dolphin noise splash' means I'm always wet
'Dolphin noise' means I love to hug
'Dolphin noise' means I'm so fucking smug
I just need something that can mend me
I'm not feeling tuna friendly

Smug fucking dolphins fucking
Smug fucking dolphins fucking dolphins
Smug fucking dolphins fucking
Smug fucking dolphins smugly bumping ugly's
I wish I was a dolphin SPLASH

FRAN: And I've tried to be more dolphin, but my sexual statistics are more like…

Countdown music plays.

SFX: 15

FRAN: Lovers penetrative-ly over

SFX: 15

FRAN: …years.

SFX: 7

FRAN: …and a half in relationships,

SFX: 7

FRAN: …and a half casual partners. His half was the casual half.

SFX: 5

FRAN: I met on the internet.

SFX: 0

FRAN: One-night stands but more…

SFX: 2

FRAN: Night stands because I often leave my phone charger at their house.

SFX: 6

FRAN: Condom fails, although if failing to wear a condom is a failure then......

SFX: Many more. 5

FRAN: STI checks, see the

SFX: 6

FRAN: …aforementioned condom fails.

SFX: 4

FRAN: Morning after pills.

SFX: 3

FRAN: Pregnancy scares.

SFX: 2

FRAN: Coils and

SFX: 1

FRAN: Awkward conversation with my mother.

FRAN: My trying to fix sex isn't a recent thing. In some ways I've been trying to fix sex ever since I was first sexually activated. I kept a diary every single day of my teenage years and I am going to read to you from that diary now. I haven't changed a word of it.

'Last Night' by The Strokes plays.

The year is 2003. Dawson's Creek has just ended and The Darkness seem like a band that are gonna go on and on forever. Sixteen-year-old Fran thinks that sex will be like the women in the Herbal Essences adverts coming under waterfalls, but Justin Timberlake is there, and Leonardo Dicaprio is posing nearby and Sarah Michelle Gellar is sticking one curious toe into my mountain stream.

FRAN *picks up her teenage diary and reads.*

FRAN: Dear diary,

Me and Lee had some serious chats and decided that we were both ready to take our relationship to the next level. So, I went down on him. Upon writing this, in hindsight, I'm unsure if I ought to have done it, as now it feels like it is all I do and I am beginning to get a sore neck. The difference is he is for sure far more AHEM turned on by it and I can bring him to AHEM climax every single time. But I don't think I've ever been close. This of course isn't his fault as I'm unsure I will ever be turned on. I'm just as I told him not wired up right. But this is not important- physicality isn't important – I love his company and that is all that matters to me. Yesterday we went to the football and after worrying that Blackburn Rovers were a rubbish team they beat Chelsea 2-1!

FRAN *dances like only a sixteen-year-old can. When* **FRAN** *stops dancing…*

FRAN: As I've been writing this show, a lot of people have asked me, "What exactly is wrong with you Fran?" and the truth is, I'm still not wired up right.

'Let's Get It On' by Marvin Gaye plays and **FRAN** *dances 'sexily'.*

FRAN: Alright! The lights are low, music is on and *we* are about to commence sex. But before we get down to it, there are just a few things you need to know.

Step one: my body. I like my body. It's a good body. I particularly like my sexy, sexy, sexy, sexy...... mind. Now, my mind is going to try and stay in the room with you, but it's also going to be thinking about how we went to the petting zoo earlier and you hand fed that goat, like you really *really* hand fed that goat and now that hand that fed that goat is sliding slowly down my body towards my *(vagina)* and I'm thinking GOAT! GOAT! GOAT! But I'm also thinking about climate change and Michael Gove *(get out of my head Michael Gove)* and what does a spleen do anyway? And I'm worrying that the sex is going to hurt.

And my ears right….

'Genie in A Bottle' by Christina Aguilera plays.

FRAN *moves to a microphone and reads from her teenage diary.*

Ok, so at first, I was sceptical as kissing ears is not the most appealing prospect, but it was the most fantastic thing. Sounds funny *(literally the ear kissing sounds hilarious in your ear)* but wow, kissing ears = amazing. I'd much prefer Lee to kiss my ear than try any kind of creativeness with his hands. Guys honestly haven't got a clue when it comes to fingering… or at least they would do if they didn't try to do it through denim.

FRAN *closes the diary with a snap and is back to talking to the audience directly.*

FRAN: But once the denim is off…

'Push the Button' by the Sugababes plays. **FRAN** *opens the glittery sparkling curtains behind her, revealing a projector screen.*

FRAN: The stage is set, your penis is in the wings, my velvet curtains start to open.

FRAN *turns on an Overhead Projector.*

FRAN: Everybody in *(name of theatre)* put your hands together and welcome to the stage, my vulva.

Huge applause from the audience as **FRAN** *reveals a clumsy but accurate drawing of her vulva.*

FRAN: So, here we have labia majora, minora, urethra, vagina and good old mons pubis. And that's my clitoris. She can be a bit above it all, doesn't always communicate with the rest of my vulva. And if we are getting up close and personal, just be aware, there can be a slight debris zone. Things my vulva has been near that day can accumulate in and around here throughout the day.

FRAN *places a key, paperclip and any other random bits of debris on the vulva on the OHP screen.*

FRAN: If anyone's lost a front door key, come and check after the show, it could be in my vulva.

And if it hurts, it's going to hurt *here…*

FRAN *points to the entrance of the vagina on screen.*

FRAN: and that's because it is dry, dry, DRY.

FRAN *places the image of a tiny camel, cactus and sombrero on the OHP.*

FRAN: And lube will help, but I'll feel a bit embarrassed because you brought your penis AND an erection, the least I could do was be lubricated for you. And it's hard to know if it hurts because I'm not turned on enough or I'm not turned on enough because I'm worrying it's going to hurt! This is turning you on, right? This is getting you ready for sex?

The music becomes military in nature.

FRAN: And if you're going in: use a protractor for a clear 125-degree entry angle. The angle that hurt less for me isn't a very friendly penis angle. And we'll do an awkward ceilidh barn dance manoeuvre, 'take your penis by the hand and swing it round and dosey-doh!' And if we haven't lost the moment, go steady at a speed of 5TPM, *(thrusts per minute)*, in and out count as TWO separate thrusts. Watch out for my coil! This one is particularly pokey. And legend has it there's a G spot, a U spot, an O spot, an A spot and a wifi hotspot…but to be honest, I'll probably ask you to stop before we need any of those. And I'll be a bit sad afterwards and feel like my vagina is the enemy and you'll be a bit sad because you'll think it's your fault.

'Let's Get It On' plays again.

FRAN: It's called FSD, female sexual dysfunction. I'm dysfunctional. Sexually. And femalely. Sexy! Ok? Ready? Lights out.

FRAN *clicks off OHP light.*

'Genie in a Bottle' plays again.

FRAN *grabs her diary and sits on the golden stool.*

FRAN: Sex attempt 6. Lee and I mentally prepared. I made a tent in the garden with 2 wooden chairs and a bed sheet, like a romantic canopy. Couldn't get it in. No sex.

Attempt 9. I made room pretty with candles, flowers and even tidied for sex with Lee...couldn't get it in. No sex.

Attempt 11. Asked Lee to put his penis in unerect and then we could kiss to make it harden inside me. Figured putting it in soft would mean no pain.

FRAN *acts out what she is describing. She is the penis.*

FRAN: But what would happen is he'd come towards me soft, get up to me, harden, not go in. So he would retreat, it'd soften and then he'd come back towards me etc etc, NO SEX. Sort of like a sexy barn dance – *(still making that same joke).*

FRAN *puts down her diary.*

FRAN: Unhelpful things people have said:

PEOPLE: "Can't you just enjoy the sex you are having? I feel satisfied knowing my partner is satisfied?" "Have you ever thought about becoming a lesbian?" "Isn't it a bit hedonistic to be seeking pleasure all the time Fran? I get a lot out of healthy debate."

FRAN: "Yeah but how's your sex life?"

PEOPLE: "No complaints." *(Dolphin noise.)*

FRAN: So, medical science has pretty much given up on me and my FSD. Female Sexual Dysfunction.

DOCTOR: "Good luck."

FRAN: There's nothing more we can do. In the past they'd suggested I just 'pop some Savlon on the problem area' or 'have a glass of wine to loosen up a bit'. Or when I was 16 even said-

DOCTOR: "You just have a very underused vagina, it's very springy, get out and use it more."

FRAN: I even asked the opinion of Dr Christian off of TV's *Embarrassing Bodies* and he said –

DR CHRISTIAN: "I don't know."

FRAN: And there are 24 approved solutions for similar disorders in men who already orgasm on average three times as much as women do during sex and it's not a competition, imagine, but Viagra has just been made available over the counter without prescription which is fantastic news for men but I've found medical research and solutions for female sexual problems are decades… lifetimes behind men's. And that is because women don't have to be aroused to have sex. Women don't have to enjoy sex to conceive. At school if we are lucky we are taught about periods, pregnancy and its prevention and there is no mention of pleasure and that is because it is not seen as necessary. Which is frightening right. We should know we are meant to enjoy it. And I guess not enjoying sex isn't life threatening, so perhaps I should just be happy with healthy debate, we could healthy debate right now?

INTERNET: "Do you want to fix Sex?"

> **FRAN** *opens and switches on the OHP. On it are Google searches for sexual wonder cures and we hear the voice of the internet…*

FRAN: "Oh hi, late night internet pop up advert."

INTERNET: "Click here Fran. We know you want to be a dolphin."

FRAN: "I do want to be a dolphin. Have you been reading my search history?"

INTERNET: "We've got supplements, procedures *(invasive and non-invasive)* and life changing miracle solutions *(some results may vary)*."

FRAN: "And it's all completely safe, tried and tested right?"

INTERNET: "Trust us Fran. We know how to make you squirt like a dolphin. Dive in. Splash."

FRAN: Click!

> *On each new verse* **FRAN** *places a new picture on the OHP, showing a different miracle cure.*

SONG: **Professional Advice**

Have you always got a headache?

Always saying 'not tonight'?
They'll put up with it for quite a bit
But then they will take flight.
You need a little boost to keep your partner
Satisfied.

If they're saying 'Oh, I'm fine with this'
- they've lied
I mean what harm can a little Google have?

Do you want to find a cure? Oh, you don't,
are you sure?

We can bring you satisfaction at a price
And though the price may seem to double
We can cure your lady trouble
If you listen to professional advice.

FRAN: *(Spoken.)* Ok so I'll try this sex liquid, I mean what could be the harm in trying a banned aphrodisiac made from the body of crushed beetles. She looks like she's having a lovely time!

FRAN *puts a sheet of acetate on the OHP with a bottle of Spanish Fly on it. It has a lady looking **very** happy on it.*

SONG: **Professional Advice** *(Continued.)*

Try some of my Spanish fly
You'll compliment this supplement and simply
have to buy

If you're craving a sensation
You'll enjoy the inflammation
It's killed a few who took it but don't let
that make you shy

> *At least you'll have amazing sex as you die*
> *You'll go out on a high*
> *With Spanish Fly*

FRAN: I actually don't want to take anything that's killed anyone. The problem probably needs more direct targeting, The O shot!

SONG: ***Professional Advice*** *(Continued.)*

> *We'll do the trick with a prick*
> *A healthy shot of plasma that will fix your*
> *issue quick.*
>
> *We can give you an injection*
> *For a feminine Herection.*
>
> *It's fifteen hundred dollars but it only*
> *takes a tick.*
>
> *You need a needle straight into your lady*
> *Dick.*
>
> *If your stomach can stick*
> *A tiny prick.*

FRAN: I don't have fifteen hundred dollars. I work in the Arts. This next one is actually literally called The Orgasmatron. I don't even need to write jokes anymore.

> **FRAN** *places a sheet of acetate on the OHP with a picture of the Orgasmatron device on it.*

SONG: ***Professional Advice*** *(Continued.)*

> *We'll give you shocks in your box*
> *Send a current to your coccyx that will*
> *knock you off your socks.*
>
> *Then you'll feel some little flickers*
> *In the gusset of your knickers*
> *The sex will be electric it'll blast you off*
> *the blocks.*

Ecstatic with the static from your firm
butt-ocks.

You'll be craving all the cocks
With our small box
Which they implant directly into your spine.

FRAN: What have these lovely men got to say for themselves eh?

FRAN *places images of a panel of male doctors on the OHP.*

SONG: ***Professional Advice*** *(Continued.)*

We'll make a slit for your clit.

FRAN: NO!!!

FRAN *closes OHP flap sharply.*

FRAN: And in late night post coital Googling I have considered all of these options. So maybe the answer isn't on the internet, maybe we just need to talk about this, normalize it.

Pub ambience music plays, full of laughs and clinks of glasses.

FRAN: Fran is having a drink with her friend Paulo.

"I don't enjoy sex the way other people seem to Paulo. Did you know the whole human genome was mapped before anyone did a detailed ultrasound of the clitoris and the clitoris isn't even in a lot of anatomy books, and did you know that in the 17th century, people thought the clitoris was a birth defect, a tiny penis, which women grew if they touched themselves. Sorry I learnt a lot of vagina facts and I've no idea how I'll fit them all into the show."

PAULO: "Hold up a second Fran. That's sad Fran, that's really sad."

FRAN: "No it's not sad, it's fine."

PAULO: "No, it's devastating. Who are you sleeping with? Amateurs! Look, I'm just saying this as a friend. And it wouldn't be weird. It wouldn't be. It wouldn't be weird Fran. But basically, there has never been woman who Paulo has not satisfied.

My name is Paulo. I love vagina. More than that I am vagina. I am the Chris Martin of vaginas. Fran, I can fix you. Just one time with me and you won't even need to do this show or I could be in the show…"

SONG: ***Magic Penis Song***

PAULO: *It's just that....*

>*Fran you put me in a difficult position*
>*Cos lord knows I ain't no physician*
>*And sure you talk about a medical condition*
>*But you should know I'm a lady parts magician.*
>
>*Other boys may have tried to enter*
>*To them I'll be a penetration mentor.*
>*We can start a vag rehab centre*
>*You should know I'm a lady parts magician…ter.*
>
>*If you do it with me*
>*Like Debbie McGee*
>*I'll make it easy like open sesame.*
>
>*My magic penis, penis, can fix you*
>*My magic penis, penis, can fix you*
>*Which cock*
>*This cock, you might get a shock cos*
>*This magic penis can fix you.*
>
>*What I'm telling you is fact not fiction.*
>*Gonna bless you with my dick benediction.*
>*All you're missing is a little bit of friction*
>*My dick can fix your lady bits affliction.*

PAULO *stands up and begins to rap.*

>*I'll pull a rabbit from your hat and you're*
>*gonna give thanks*
>*Cos the rabbit is my dick and the hat is my pants.*
>*I got powers like the ancient druids I'll be*

all up in your henge with my healing fluids.
I'll take you to the peak
To the peak of the mountain.
I'm gonna dribble like a champagne fountain
And when I get you out of your Gryffindor
pyjamas I'll wave my wand and you'll
expelliarmus.

I know what makes you tick Fran.
I can make you Fran tick.
I put the man in the middle of romantic
Stand back Fran, this is going to be gigantic
I'll make you wet like, like the Atlantic.
I'll make like Houdini embrace your bikini,
You're gonna explode like Santorini
So rub my lamp because my Jism is a genie
I'll be the crème fresh in your buckwheat blini.

PAULO *goes into the audience.*

My dick is magnificent
Might even be omnipotent.
Don't be ambivalent
A miracle is imminent
The minute I apply my dick to your predicament.

PAULO *approaches an audience member.*

PAULO: Hey there my name is Paulo, may I apply my dick to your predicament please?

SONG: ***Magic Penis Song*** *(Continued.)*

My magic penis
It's a divining stick
With a bag of tricks.
It brings good karma
It's the snake and the charmer.
An interior designer
I'll rearrange your vagina.

Dick my dick, yeah that'll do the trick, yeah
My magic penis will fix you.

PAULO: "I think that's done the trick. I'm just going to go for a wee."

FRAN *speaks to the audience.*

FRAN: I wish I could say that I have never taken the offer of a Magic Penis up and it's hard to know what to say when they ask… "How was THAT for you?"

'Genie in a Bottle' by Christina Aguilera plays again and **FRAN** *walks over to her teenage diary.*

FRAN: Dear diary,

Lee seems to be loving learning the art of foreplay…which is the bit before the sex. Ok, I'd never fake anything but sometimes I may emphasise my enthusiasm when he's down there just because it boosts his confidence and I can see how happy it makes him and I don't want us both to feel like total failures. It is very rewarding to be able to give something like that to your loved one and for them to really enjoy it. Today I had my first ever detention, but Lee had one too, both were hungry afterwards, we had Nando's.

FRAN *puts the diary down.*

FRAN: When I was 21, I read a boyfriend's diary, that I'm pretty sure he left out and open for me to read, and he said "I think the sex is bad". And I was devastated. They *have* to be enjoying it, the only enjoyment I get from it is that they are having a lovely time, if they aren't enjoying it then what's the point?

So what I've said to every lover I've had is:

SONGS: **Best at Sex & I've Disappeared**

> *You're the best at sex*
> *You're the best at sex*
> *You're the worst at being bad at sex.*
>
> *Your sex got an A* at GCSE*
> *Your sex got an NVQ and a BTEC level 3*
> *Your sex deserves an honorary degree.*

But not from the university of me
My department of sexology was ruined by
Austerity.
So, you see it's not you it's me.

So, tell me when it's over, when your bits
complete
You pick up the pace and I sink into the
Sheets.

My bodies in the room
But my minds no longer here
You think we're connecting but I've
Disappeared.

You make love to the mattress like it's a
martial art.
I feel like an actress phoning in my part
You whisper "you feel good"
Too close to my ear.
You think that I've heard you but I've
Disappeared.
I've disappeared, I've disappeared

I think that you think that I feel what you're
feeling
But I've slipped out of the bed and I'm
perching on the ceiling.
I'm looking down on you making love to the
pillow slip.
I bide my time as you tighten your grip.

You're racing to the end but I'm not coming
with you.

It seems this is a game designed for one and not for two.
I try to find the words that you long to hear
I don't want to tell you but I've disappeared.

FRAN: So I thought, no more being passive. No more having sex because it seems like the right thing or the nice thing or the convenient thing to do.

From now on I was only going to have No Lies Sex. Or rebrand FSD as FAKE. SEX. DON'T! I'm not going to be a performing seal balancing a ball on the end of its nose, or a dolphin jumping for fish. I am not Free Willy. Because normally sex with me is a little bit like-

'Le Freak' by Chic plays and **FRAN** *does an elaborate and funky sex dance routine, complete with noises of wild abandon. Once the routine is complete, she goes to the microphone.*

FRAN: The next man I slept with was going to be a very lucky man indeed, he was getting total honesty. Rule 1 of No Lies Sex – No making this noise anymore *(PORN NOISE)* Or pretending to be a dolphin *(DOLPHIN NOISE)*. Ok next lover, let's go!

FRAN *does the same dance routine, full of energy but entirely silent. It is weird and empty.* **FRAN** *goes to microphone.*

FRAN: Rule 2 of No Lies Sex. No pulling sex faces, unless they pull themselves.

FRAN *does same dance routine but with blank bemused befuddled face.*

FRAN: And it wasn't nearly as fun as I make it look.

FRAN *dances unenthusiastically. Eventually the dancing turns into small pelvic thrusts, suggesting sex.*

FRAN: And he asks "please may I come?" and I say "please". Please. And he does. And I get sad. And he feels like a failure and so he does the gentlemanly thing and ends up falling asleep fingering me. A lot of men have fallen asleep fingering me. And in the dark I realize that I regularly have sex that I do not entirely want. And I choose to have sex that makes me feel alone, rather than being on my own and I stop telling them it hurts because it hurts them too much. I am tired of feeling difficult, and complicated and like hard work and No Lies Sex didn't work, the doctors didn't work. Magic Peni do not work. And I could just not have sex like the doctor said, but I want to feel alive and free and connected and loved and good. So, if there is a god of sex and pleasure, of dolphin desire help me now.

A dramatic thunder roll.

FRAN: Ok, I need you to use your imagination here. In an ideal world we'd have the clouds parting. A choir of singing porpoises descending from the back of the theatre, an enormous beam of light and a huge slippery fin poking down through the clouds.

DOLPHIN GOD: "You called?"

FRAN *speaks to the* **DOLPHIN GOD** *as if it is above her in the sky.*

FRAN: "Dolphin god of desire?"

DOLPHIN GOD: "The very same."

FRAN: "I want to fix sex."

DOLPHIN GOD: "Don't give up Fran. We know a place for you."

FRAN: "Where?"

DOLPHIN GOD: "Sex Camp."

FRAN: "Sex Camp?"

DOLPHIN GOD: "Sex Camp."

FRAN: "Where is this magical camp of sex?"

DOLPHIN GOD: "Dorset. Just off the M3. Turn right at the Little Chef."

FRAN *speaks to the audience.*

FRAN: So I told you at the beginning that I would let you know if any of this is not true, and this...this *is* true...well I didn't have a divine intervention from a bottlenose dolphin god, but I did go to sex camp. This place exists, this happened, it is weirdly near a Little Chef. Ticket booked. The website says I can learn hugging for beginners, kissing with fire and advanced cervical orgasm with fire.

SEX CAMP: The only rules are no spanking and no repressing your urges.

FRAN: I Googled "Is this a cult?"...and Google said "probably not", so I packed one pair of dungarees, because they add a bit of mystery to where exactly my genitals might be at any one time. Like they should be here, but they could be here. Or here. Or here.

SEX CAMP: "Please bring your own sheets as we can't change the bedding fast enough for the rate of ejaculations, male and female."

FRAN: Anti-bacterial hand rub.

SEX CAMP: "Remember no booze. No drugs. Just love. Have a juicy day."

FRAN: And off I go with my friend's parting words ringing in my ears:

FRIEND: "Don't let them finger you Fran!"

FRAN: And I'm thinking don't worry, I won't, no way. Don't get fingered.

'I Like To Move It' by Reel 2 Real plays.

FRAN: And this is genuinely the song that's playing when I arrive at Sex Camp and people are telling me I'm brave and bold for coming on my own, but all I've done is come to a camp devoted to sex, as a sexually dysfunctional, femalely dysfunctional woman at Sex Camp.

SEX CAMP: "I promise that I will not do anything I do not want to do but I will do anything that I do want to do."

FRAN: So I stay in a single sex dorm and there are three workshops every day, and I am like a tiny baby salmon trying to swim upstream towards dolphin lagoon.

SEX CAMP: "Workshop 1. Hugging-"

FRAN: A gentle start.

SEX CAMP: "Align your genitals. Three deep breaths. You'll know when to end..."

FRAN: Turns out I do not know when to end! No one wants to be the dick who ends the hug.

SEX CAMP: "Workshop 2. Being Naked."

FRAN: "Do I have to be naked for the being naked workshop?" Backpack off. I try not to look at everyone's bits but there are bits everywhere, bits, bits, bits..."

SEX CAMP: "Workshop 3, Energetic sex-"

FRAN: FINALLY SEX.

> **FRAN** *begins to wave her arms with a great deal of intensity.*

FRAN: Actually, I hadn't worked out that *energetic* sex doesn't mean athletic sex.

> It means sex using your energetic field. So, I end up shagging a man in the heart with my imaginary energetic penis. My partner loved it, turns out I'm a very talented *energetic* lover. We are encouraged to imagine our energetic penis's. Mine is pale, thin and flaccid.

> **FRAN** *goes to microphone to speak*

FRAN: "Erm hi, Sex Camp? Sorry, when do we get to the actual sex? It's called SEX camp. Y'know *(Sings.)* "Penetration Times, C'mon". I've only got 4 days to fix sex."

SEX CAMP: "We'd like to remind campers that penetration is not encouraged at sex camp. If you really need to penetrate-"

FRAN: "I really do."

SEX CAMP: "You can do that at the Cock Inn."

FRAN: So for context, it was really called the Cock Inn and it was-

SEX CAMP: "A caravan to the left of the car park."

FRAN: "I don't think you've quite understood, I'm here to fix sex, y'know SEX."

> *(To audience.)* And I stormed off to my next workshop and stumble into –

SEX CAMP: "Welcome to the Love Lounge."

FRAN: And there is a man being tickled with a feather on my left, and his girlfriend is having her toes sucked on my right. And it's just bodies *everywhere* and they sound like they are having a really lovely time. And I want that. And none of these people were at the energetic sex class. And no one is doing this…

> **FRAN** *mimics penetrative sex with her hands.*

FRAN: Day three and I am in. I walk like this…

FRAN *floats across the stage, blowing bubbles as she does so.*

FRAN: I lick a man's face like I'm a dog, because that's what he wants and I am cool with that. And I get tickled for ten minutes solidly because it turns out, who knew, consensual tickling is what I want. I couldn't quite bring myself to call my vagina a *Yoni,* although that was better than calling it 'source of life place and sacred space'. And this might be an over-share but you've seen the debris that accumulates in my vagina...I was for the first time in a long time, really, really, really wet. Gushing. I was in the same pool as the dolphins and I was clapping along like a happy seal. Yes! Yes! Yes!

SEX CAMP: "Thank you for your time at Sex Camp. Please leave the camp now."

FRAN: "Oh no, it's not time to leave yet. I've only just started functioning. Can I stay a few more days?"

SEX CAMP: "Please leave the camp now."

FRAN: "I haven't actually used my new dolphin powers for good yet. I haven't even wrapped a squid or an eel around my-"

SEX CAMP: "Please leave the camp now."

FRAN *talks to the audience.*

FRAN: I'd booked for four days. Those four days were up. I wanted to stay longer, but there were no more beds. And at this point I really should have packed up my things and gone home. But I went and bought a tent. The only tent on sale in that small, small Dorset town. It was red.

Beyonce's 'Crazy in Love' plays.

FRAN *pops her red tent and struts to a microphone.*

FRAN: "Hello fellow sex camper with whom I've developed a connection. I'm staying an extra week and I've got a lovely tent. I know penetration isn't really encouraged here but I'm functioning. We have a small wet window in which to penetrate. Would you like to come back to my tent? For some penetration!"

SONG: **_Nasty in Namaste_**

My chakras are balanced the stars are
Aligned.
Tonight in my tent we are gonna go all the
Way.
We are gonna levitate as we bump and grind
And put the nasty back in Namaste.

We are 90 minutes in and we haven't even
touched
Except for when I poked your aura too much.
We were staring in each other's eyes the whole
Time.
You bang a tiny gong and I finger a wind
Chime.

Mmm not a cult, not a cult, not a cult but if
it is a cult then cool it's a cool cult.
Not a cult, not a cult, not a cult.
Who you calling a cult?

Wait, we should cloth your penis in it's
ritual robes.

The Durex condom in my hand
is a little untantric and completely off
brand.

We should use the leaf of an old oak tree
But actually that doesn't protect us from
having a baby....or STI's....so no oak leaves please. Thanks.
What would you suggest lover?

Goat skin?... That's not a condom.
Rain?... Not a condom.
Quinoa?... Not a condom.
Breath?...not a contraceptive mate, don't even try it.

My chakras are balanced the stars are aligned
Tonight in my tent we are gonna go all the
Way.

We are gonna levitate as we bump and grind
And put the nasty back in Namaste.

FRAN'S LOVER: "You are bending back my penis at a funny angle and it's sort of painful."

FRAN: I've never cried during sex before, afterwards sure, all the time, but never mid-way through. And he says –

FRAN'S LOVER: "This is beautiful."

FRAN: And I say – "I thought it was gonna work this time. I did everything right. We looked into each other's eyes, we didn't touch for ages, you saw my aura *(you said it was orange which is frankly quite disappointing)* but something still went wrong. Maybe I'm just not meant to have sex."

And so, we lay there listening to the sounds of other people having dolphin fun all around us, and I wanted to leave the next morning. My confidence was knocked, my blowhole was blocked, my flippers were fingers again. But I had committed to Sex Camp, so I threw myself into the next few days.

On the last day is the most popular class. It had been fully booked my entire stay and a space became available. This was my chance, because if I couldn't fix sex at Sex Camp where could I fix sex?

Spiritual music plays and **FRAN** *goes to stage right mic stand. She becomes the workshop leader.*

LEADER: "I invite the worshipper to gaze upon Yoni."

FRAN: It's a Yoni Worshipping workshop. A vagina worshipping workshop. Imagine, I'm lying down in a room of about 30 couples, and we each have a partner gazing at our vagina.

LEADER: "Men, describe what you can see."

FRAN: And the man worshipping my vag says

MAN: "Yoni's made a little bubble."

LEADER: "Men, place one finger at the entrance of Yoni and ask for verbal and physical consent. Let Yoni suck you in."

FRAN: And I'm panicking because Yoni had never sucked anything in in her life. Except for once a Halls Soother… I'd read in *Cosmopolitan* Magazine, a really reputable source, that a menthol sweet in a partner's mouth could enhance oral. It doesn't, it burns, please do not try that at home.

LEADER: "Does Yoni say yes?"

FRAN: So Yoni and me both say

FRIEND: "Don't let them finger you Fran!"

FRAN: "Sorry friend from home." And I am like a giant finger puppet on the hand of this man and all of the men in the room are crying.

LEADER: "Yessss, it can be emotional, paying attention to something you may have rushed by or treated badly in the past."

FRAN: The man with his finger in my vag nods. It is probably the longest time anyone has ever looked at my vagina, longer than a doctor and definitely longer than me.

LEADER: "Men, describe this experience, how is this for you?"

FRAN: A smattering of…

MEN: "Spiritual, connection, love, holy, beautiful, connected."

FRAN: Goes around the room and the man attached to the finger in my vag says:

MAN: "A REVERENTIAL HOMECOMING!"

FRAN: And I like, "WHAT, my vagina is –"

MAN: "A REVERENTIAL HOMECOMING."

LEADER: "Women, listen to your Yoni's, tune in to what she is saying."

FRAN: And I'm panicking because Yoni doesn't speak, that's the problem. Yoni is silent and I'm going to have to make something up, something as good as –

MAN: "A REVERENTIAL HOMECOMING."

FRAN: Something like Yoni says "Give penis a chance" or "Yoni says phone home" or "Yoni says-"

FRAN *climbs inside her tent. The tent becomes a talking vagina!*

YONI: "Frances!"

FRAN: "Yoni?"

YONI: "Frances!!!"

FRAN: "Yes?"

YONI: "THIS IS YONI."

FRAN: "The voice of my vagina?"

YONI: "My name is Yoni."

FRAN: "Are you speaking to me through my actual labia lips?"

(To audience.) I should say I have slightly dramatized this section. This conversation did happen, but I didn't actually climb inside my own vagina. That's the magic of theatre.

YONI: "You want to know how to fix sex Frances?"

FRAN: "Yes, so much Yoni, I want to be a dolphin so flipping badly."

YONI: "You want to know how to graduate from yoni-veristy?"

FRAN: "I want to graduate from yoni-versity and then do some night school and then maybe a doctorate."

YONI: "You won't like it."

FRAN: "Hey, that's a bit presumptuous."

YONI: "Ok. Nothing more."

FRAN: "Yup I'm listening, I'm not going to say anything more, you talk I listen, that's the deal."

YONI: "Nothing More! Unless it's special."

FRAN: "Woah Yoni! That is not a good message and I have it on very good authority that you are meant to be a –"

YONI: "A reverential homecoming, I know."

FRAN: Yoni, could you scroll down a bit, there must be a footnote or something."

YONI: "No footnote. Good luck! Also, please only wear cotton pants and get a Mooncup if you can't use the correct absorbency of tampon."

FRAN bursts out of tent, she is wearing a full dolphin costume. She starts to put down the pop-up tent.

FRAN: No, no, no, no, no! Thanks Yoni, that's just not going to work. Because special means love and I am not *in love* and special means time and I don't always have time for special. I've barely enough time to attempt and give up on a wank whilst microwaving a jacket potato...don't tell me "you should lovingly bake your potato", what if I want instant mash? And if Yoni is right, the most awful thing about this is that *they* were right, the people who said wait for the right person, that sex is much better once you're in love, the people who said 'stop having sex like a lad Fran' or that I'm having too much sex or not enough sex, or too bland or too wild or too much sex with men who work in the Arts. That last one is true.

And if Yoni is right, I have to slow down and be with just myself and my body and I have never wanted to do that.

FRAN sits on her compressed tent.

FRAN: When I came back to London everything had dried up. My tank was drained. I tried energetic sexting with someone from Sex Camp but my energetic phallus wouldn't stretch to Winchester. I stopped trying to fix sex.

When I stopped trying to have sex, things did start to happen. I'm not having sex, 'unless it's special' but special doesn't have to mean *love* or even lighting a single tealight. It means only having sex when I want to, and only with people I really want to have sex with, who won't be offended if I say 'no', 'stop' or 'how about we try it like this?'. Which sounds really basic, but I so often break those rules. And being ok-ish being on my own and being completely honest-ish with myself.

'Last Nite' by The Strokes plays and **FRAN** *walks to pick up her teenage diary.*

FRAN: Last night, I made love to the most caring, special person I have ever met. It was totally unplanned. On the 30th June 2003, Lee and I had sex, whilst a small black cat watched us. We maintained eye contact throughout. Afterwards I insisted he have a cigarette like in the movies and also more than that, I wanted to commemorate the event, so I gave him a 2 pence coin to keep with him always, as a sort of war medallion to honour the battle he had valiantly fought against my hymen.

FRAN *walks to middle of the stage, still holding her diary*

FRAN: That's what I wrote in my diary anyway but in reality losing my virginity was painful, was over very quickly and Lee dumped me the week after.

And I wish I could tell 16-year-old Fran that at 31 she had fixed sex. And I wish I could give her the tools to stop her from disappearing in bed for all those years. And I wish that she could know that even though she feels like she's on her own with this, she isn't. Because yeah, some people are just sexual legends, dolphins, but most of us will have, or be with someone who has a sexual difficulty at some point. So, this is where I am at today and the truth is I haven't got an answer, I haven't fixed sex. I was really hoping I'd have a nice big ejaculatory ending to this show for you all. I bought a confetti cannon, for y'know KAPOW. I wrote a finale song, "Now that I'm a fucking smug dolphin"... it's essentially a remix of the first song. And a show needs a happy ending right?

FRAN *slowly takes off dolphin costume.*

FRAN: But the way things 'traditionally' end isn't going to happen for me, yet, and actually that's ok. But we don't have to end this show like everyone else. We can end in our own way and finish at our own pace.

Women vaginally lubricate every time they are praised. I'm just going to leave that thought with you.

FRAN *walks over to the confetti cannon and explodes it above her head.*

THE AUDIENCE

After performances of *Ad Libido*, I invited the audience to write down one thing they wish they had known about sex, their body or relationships at 16 years old. The answers were honest, moving and hugely relatable. These are some of the responses…

- If you aren't into them, you don't have to stay

- Actually talk to who you are getting down with, it makes it so much more fun.

- It won't happen for a while, but don't worry. Take your time. Be patient. It isn't a race.

- Don't ever pretend you are enjoying it. Be honest and talk, talk, talk.

- Don't worry about matching underwear. Clothes never come off in the right order to see it.

- Sex can be messy and awkward, so it's good to do it with someone you can laugh with.

- Sex does not = put penis in vagina. Those textbooks got it wrong.

- Worry less about how you make them feel by saying no.

- You are worthy of feeling sexy and having sex just as you are.

- It gets a lot less scary when you've figured out you like girls (and better too).

- Find a lover who doesn't define sex as purely penetration.

- Your pleasure is as important as theirs.

- You are not boring for asking them to wear a condom

- Give yourself a helping hand.

- Be yourself in bed.

- You'll have it when you have it. Chill the fuck out!

- It's okay to wait. Just because all your friends are doing it, doesn't mean you should rush. You'll know!

- Take your socks off first.

- If he doesn't appreciate a full bush, he isn't worth it.

- Don't worry, it's called a queef.

- This sex stuff will get better when you dump him.

- It's about your internal environment, not your external environment. Cushions on the floor are not going to make it good.

- You don't have to pretend you've had sex before.

- Humour should always be dry, sex doesn't have to be.

- Focus on developing all parts of your life, not just doing well in school. Relationships are important and your pleasure is important.

- Everyone else says they are having it – don't feel the pressure to conform! It turns out most of them are making it up and are as scared as you.

- You can't catch talent from sex.

- It IS ok just to hug.

- Relax…breathe. You're amazing. Cuddle LOTS. It's ok to say NO.

- Don't sleep with boring men, straight girls or boys in sixth form.

- You won't be alone forever.

- Don't feel weird about your sexuality. Sapiosexuality is a real thing and its ok to take some time to figure it out.

- Only sleep with people who make you feel good about yourself and laugh lots when you're doing it. Sex is awkward, find the fun.

- Be honest. The person you are with is as scared as you. Also, one day podcasts will be invented and they are almost as good as sex.

- Chill the fuck out, you have the rest of your life to have sex.

- Don't rush it. You don't have to be like everyone else. The right time will come.

- Girls are just as fun as boys, nicer too and can give tampons when you need them.

- Own your awkwardness and don't apologise so much.

- Follow your own path. Fuck what everyone else thinks.

- Alcohol is not necessary for sex.

- It's ok to say what you mean, so don't be chicken.

- You're allowed to enjoy it too.

- Love yourself like a full-time job. Stop living your life for others. You are a powerful woman.

- I know you are scared and you are going to be scared for a while. You will feel like you're not enough, broken and owe them their pleasure.

Eventually you will start learning how to own your experience. And you are not alone. Hang in there and be true to yourself.

- Guilt is bullshit and will hold you back.

- The penis goes INSIDE.

- The girl has to finish too.

- Serious conversations aren't automatically unsexy.

- You can ask for what you want. You can tell him if you're not enjoying it.

- It doesn't matter what other people think of you.

- The friends you have now are the ones you'll value most in 40 years. LOOK AFTER THEM.

- You are supposed to enjoy it. You are allowed to say no.

- It's not all about him. You are enough. Ps stop faking!

- Don't take the evil contraceptive pill just because you're led to believe it's the only real option and will give you 'clear skin' – it isn't and it probably won't.

- Say no, say yes, but say it with conviction and only if you believe it.

- Don't do what everyone else is doing. They are idiots.

- Don't lie to your girlfriends about how it went. It's not a competition. Level the playing field.

- It's not all about the boys.

- It's ok to connect your body and your mind.

- You don't need to feel ashamed.

- You'll have it eventually.

- Take things at your own pace. It doesn't matter what other people in your year are doing.

- Don't believe anything you see on the internet.

- It's always worth the wait.

- You don't need to use sex as currency. You are enough, no matter what they think.

- Remember to live in the present. Worrying is a waste of time.

- Don't give up when it gets hard, it's so so worth it.

- The clitoris is so much bigger than you think.

- The 'come hither' gesture works wonders.

- It will be a little while before you get into your sex life stride. Don't worry – it will be fine!

- It's ok to stop when it hurts.

- Don't listen to boys when they say girls can't masturbate. You can and you love it!

- Don't pluck your eyebrows off. Bronzer is not foundation.

- You have so much fun ahead of you… don't worry!

- Sex doesn't have to equal penetration.

- Your body is a temple. Peer pressure can SUCK IT.

- Sex isn't like that scene on the Titanic, especially for the first TEN YEARS.

- When giving a blow job, don't blow, suck!

- It's normal! You're normal! There's nothing wrong with you.

- Pubic hair is gr8.

- Wank.

- Sex isn't just for men. Talk to your friends. Don't panic about not knowing anything at all.

- Don't worry about your lack of experience – you have a clitoris and you will find it soon.

- Sex is as much about intimacy as the act.

- Your vulva is perfect.

- Like a fine wine, your sex life will mature and improve. Trust me.

- Masturbate. It's great. Penetrative sex is so overrated.

- Your heart is going to break, but it's going to mend too.

- Your body is beautiful and perfectly okay as it is.

- Don't be afraid to explore your body and express your needs.

- You are fabulous, but don't yet know it.

- You'll get over him, I promise.

- Virginity is a social construct. Lube is GREAT.

- Sex is not just reproduction.

- Don't shave your legs.

- Explore your sexuality on your own first.

- It's ok to be different. You are not strange or annoying. You will find your kind of people.

- Take risks, don't be afraid of rejection. You are great.

- Don't use Sudocrem – you have thrush.

- You weren't crazy. It was the pill that messed with your emotions.

- Don't promise 'forever'.

- Stop using your parents' electric toothbrush to masturbate with.

- No one will make you as happy as your sea view and your dog do.

- You're perfect this way.

- If it feels icky, it's ok to stop.

- You are allowed to be picky about who you fancy, there's nothing wrong with you.

- Touch yourself when you are sleeping with them. I promise they don't mind.

- Go on top.

- You are a beautiful person, believe in yourself as you are enough. Also, buy new dancing shoes.

- You are more important than World of Warcraft.

- You don't have to start having sex at 16 just because it is legal.

- Women can masturbate too. Don't wait until you're 19 to figure that out.

- You will not be able to pull off faking orgasms for the rest of your life. You will have to tell him and he will not be angry. Not being able to orgasm (yet) doesn't stop you from being sexy, desirable, valuable. You deserve to feel good about your body. You can and you will.

- You don't have to shave your pubes off if you don't want to.

- Don't settle. There is someone out there who matches you.

- Be wary of mixing sex and alcohol. Sober you probably won't approve.

- I wish I'd known that sex was something for me to enjoy.

- Focus on school hun.

- There's nothing wrong with being different – kinks are good, find your people.

- It's ok to be clever as fuck.

- Stop giving a shit what other people think of you!

- Stop trying to fit in, everyone around you is a moron.

- Make sure your partner is kind and compassionate and the power balance is 50:50.

- You are not Anthony Keidis.

- I was expert enough.

- Two balls are more than enough.

- You'll find your tribe soon.

- It's ok that you literally fancy no one at school.

- Blow jobs are not boob jobs.

- Don't have sex on gravel.

- It's ok to be attracted to girls too. Don't have sex just to please a man. Explore your vagina. Ps you are AWESOME.

- Be wild and brave. Explore. You are beautiful.

- Buy a rabbit sooner. Also, go to Camp America as a coach – even though he tells you not to.

- Be nicer to your friends

- Masturbate (regularly) and get to know your body.

- Stop worrying about acne and boys.

- It's ok to have your heart broken.

- It's ok for people not to like you and for you to not like people.

- A full set of GCSE's is way cooler than a boyfriend.

- Don't bunk off school and go to the nightclub, it will change your life.

- Radiohead will still be cool in 21 years time.

- Sex will get much better when you feel into what you want and listen to the things that turn you on…and it's ok if that is women.

- It ain't gonna work first time.

- Don't shave your arms or obsess over your pubic hair.

- Having a side parting is not a personality.

- Eat more jelly babies and laugh more – this is the best bit.

- They are as nervous as you are.

- Don't listen to Christian, he is a dickhead.

- Don't be embarrassed or ashamed of your boobs.

- You're beautiful, don't put up with rubbish boyfriends.

- If you have to chase after him, leave him.

- Don't take advice from Cosmopolitan.

- Never scrimp on buying sex toys, the money is always worth it.

- Don't let them call you A-cup.

- Get him to go down on you! Also, threesomes are fun.

- Sex is not a sin and you deserve to be loved.

- It's ok to not be interested in sex yet.

- 'The Bill' isn't a good background to your first sexual experience.

- Don't worry, you are not going to die, it's called a UTI.

- Every single thing will be better from now on. Ps touch yourself.

- You don't have to carry on just because you have started.

- You will be fine and what you feel is ok.

- You can be sexually attracted to people without being emotionally attracted.

- Don't have sex with anyone who doesn't think you are the shit.

- You're gay as fuck (and that is ok).

- Love doesn't equal sex.

- Girls wank too.

- It is ok to not be ok.

- Your worth is not linked to your sexuality. You will be so much happier once you stop trying to live up to expectations and just let your true self out.

- Have an explore down there.

- Everyone is entitled to their own pleasure and body.

- Knowing where your hotspots are, e.g. your nips, is very important.

- Communication is the key.

- People will fancy you.

- Your first time will be rubbish but it will get better.

- You can get everything you want to ask for. In fact, you will.

- At 30 you still won't have had sex yet, but surprise, you feel as sexy and in love with your body and life like never before.

- The orgasms you give yourself are better than anyone else can give you.

- Learn how to put on a condom properly.

- When you are a teenager you desperately want to be the same, but all the things that make you different are the things everyone will love you for… especially yourself.

- Your cave with many ferns is loved like nothing else…let it grow.

- Your family and friends one day will completely understand your sexuality

- It's ok to not be perfect, no one is.

- You are not going to get any taller, but that's ok, you'll grow in so many other ways.

- You don't have to enjoy anal sex just because you are gay. Sucking dick is fine.

- Masturbate every day.

- Sex isn't everything but it shouldn't be bad.

- No, you are not done yet, no, you do not have to get back to the party.

- Not having a date to the prom is waaaay less embarrassing than going with Edmund would have been.

Feel free to send me yours @franbushe

9 781914 228476